LET'S EXPLORE LIFE SCIENCE

Exploring the CLASSIFICATION of LIVING THINGS

Ella Hawley

PowerKiDS press.

New York

Published in 2013 by The Rosen Publishing Group, Inc.
29 East 21st Street, New York, NY 10010

First Edition

Editor: Jennifer Way
Book Design: Kate Laczynski

Photo Credits: Cover (main, butterfly, gull), pp. 6, 7, 9 (top, bottom), 10, 11 (top), 12, 14, 15 (top), 16–17 Shutterstock.com; pp. 4–5 Ryan McVay/Lifesize/Thinkstock; p. 5 © www.iStockphoto.com/Kim Gunkel; p. 8 © www.iStockphoto.com/stane_c; p. 11 (bottom) iStockphoto/Thinkstock; p. 13 Thomas Northcut/Lifesize/Thinkstock; p. 15 (bottom) Hemera/Thinkstock; p. 16 (inset) CMSP/Getty Images; p. 18 Dr. T. J. Beveridge/Getty Images; p. 19 Wim van Egmond/Visuals Unlimited, Inc./Getty Images; p. 20 by Kate Laczynski; p. 22 © Corbis/SuperStock.

Library of Congress Cataloging-in-Publication Data

Hawley, Ella.
 Exploring the classification of living things / by Ella Hawley. — 1st ed.
    p. cm. — (Let's explore life science)
Includes index.
ISBN 978-1-4488-6172-9 (library binding) — ISBN 978-1-4488-6302-0 (pbk.) — ISBN 978-1-4488-6303-7 (6-pack)
1. Biology—Classification—Juvenile literature. I. Title.
QH83.H39 2013
570.1′2—dc23
                                    2011029885

Manufactured in the United States of America

CPSIA Compliance Information: Batch #SW12PK: For Further Information contact Rosen Publishing, New York, New York at 1-800-237-9932

CONTENTS

That's Classified!

Trees are living things. One way to classify trees is by whether they have needles or leaves. The tree shown here grows leaves.

Have you ever sorted things based on color, shape, or size? When you sort things into groups like this, you are classifying them. Scientists classify, too. They do this to make it easier to study and understand our world.

One way to classify our world is to divide things into groups based on whether they are living or nonliving. Animals are living things, while rocks are nonliving. Living things need energy to live. Living things grow, **reproduce**, **adapt** to changes in the environment, and die. Nonliving things may move or change over time, too. They do not need energy, though, nor do they reproduce or die.

Rocks are an example of nonliving things.

Species

The goal of classifying living things is to sort them into smaller and smaller groupings until that grouping is made up of only one kind of living thing. **Species** is the name for the grouping of only one kind of living thing.

For example, monkey is a general name for a type of animal. There are about 264 different species of monkeys. An emperor tamarin is a different species of monkey from a pig-tailed macaque. These two monkeys have things in common, but they have the most things in common with other members of their species.

The emperor tamarin (left) lives in South America, while the pig-tailed macaque (right) lives in Asia. These two species of monkeys are more different from each other than they are from members of their own species.

Domains and Kingdoms

Flowering plants belong to the plant kingdom and the Eukarya domain.

We are going to take a look at how scientists classify living things. All living things in the world are broken into three domains and six kingdoms. Domains are the biggest groups. The six kingdoms are the next biggest classification groupings.

The first two domains, Bacteria and Archaea, each contain one kingdom. These kingdoms have the same name as their domains. The Bacteria and Archaea domains are single-celled **organisms** that do not have a **nucleus**, or center. Eukarya is the third domain. All of the organisms in this domain have cells with a nucleus. Eukarya contains the protist, plant, fungus, and animal kingdoms.

(Right) Fish belong to the animal kingdom. (Below) Mold is part of the fungus kingdom.

About the Animal Kingdom

The kingdom with which you may be the most familiar is the animal kingdom. That is because we are part of it! Humans are part of a **class** of animals called mammals. Mammals are animals that have hair, breathe air, and feed milk to their young. Some well-known mammals are dogs, giraffes, and monkeys.

Owls are part of the bird class of animals. Birds are feathered, warm-blooded animals that lay eggs.

The animal kingdom also includes other classes of animals, such as insects, sponges, reptiles, amphibians, and birds. The animal kingdom can be grouped into animals with backbones, such as lions, snakes, and birds, and those without. Animals without backbones include bees, worms, and sea stars.

Chameleons are lizards that belong to the reptile class of animals. Reptiles are cold-blooded, scaly animals.

Sheep are just one of the more than 4,000 species of mammals on Earth.

What About Plants?

Cherry trees are seed plants. They have flowers that bloom in the spring.

The plant kingdom includes trees, flowers, ferns, and mosses. Plants make their own food through **photosynthesis**.

There are different ways to classify plants. Plants can be grouped by whether they are **vascular** or nonvascular. Vascular plants are plants that have tubelike systems for carrying water. Nonvascular plants do not have these systems. Flowering plants, trees, and ferns are vascular plants. Mosses, liverworts, and hornworts are nonvascular plants.

Plants can also be grouped based on how they reproduce. There are seed plants, such as fir trees and flowering plants. There are also plants that reproduce through **spores**. These include mosses and ferns.

You can see two different classifications of plants in this picture. The trees are vascular plants. The moss growing on the rocks is a nonvascular plant.

What Are Fungi?

Honey mushrooms are parasitic fungi that feed on tree roots.

The fungus kingdom includes mushrooms, mold, and yeast. You might think fungi are plants. They are not. Fungi cannot make their own food, as plants do.

Fungi have an important job. They are **decomposers**. Some fungi decompose, or break down, dead matter. Others are **parasites** that decompose living matter.

Most fungi have many cells. Their cells look a bit like plant cells. They are made out of the same matter that makes up the outsides of insects' bodies, though.

"Toadstool" is a word sometimes used for mushrooms that are poisonous to humans. Fly agaric, shown here, is a species of mushroom that is poisonous to humans.

Yeasts are single-celled fungi. They are used in making bread and beer.

So Many Bacteria

Bacteria can be found everywhere on Earth, from the bottoms of the oceans to the tops of mountains. They even live inside your body!

There are three main kinds of bacteria that make up this kingdom. The first group is made up of bacteria that need **oxygen** to live. The next group includes those that cannot live around oxygen. The third group is the bacteria that like oxygen but can live without it.

Lactobacillus bulgaricus (green) and *Streptococcus thermophilus* (pink) are bacteria that people use to make yogurt.

Staphylococcus aureus (blue) is a bacteria that is harmful to people. It can cause many different kinds of infections.

Scientists also classify this kingdom into groups based on how the bacteria get their energy. Some bacteria can make their own food. Other kinds get their energy by breaking down matter from living things.

Archaea and Protists

Natronococcus are in the Archaea domain. This group of organisms lives in extremely salty environments.

Like bacteria, the Archaea kingdom is made up of single-celled living things. These organisms are not the same as bacteria, though. The differences between them led scientists to make Archaea its own domain. These living things are found in some of the most extreme places on Earth, including super salty water and hot springs.

Protists are organisms that are hard to classify with any other kingdom. In fact, scientists today are thinking about ways to reclassify this kingdom into a number of new kingdoms. Scientists often use the term protists to talk about organisms that are in the Eukarya domain that are not plants, animals, or fungi.

The amoeba is a protist that moves by changing the shape of its body. It stretches one part and the rest of the cell follows.

Break It Down!

After an organism has been classified into a kingdom, scientists classify it into smaller groups until it is classified into a species. Some classification groupings have a subgroup, which breaks that grouping into smaller but closely related groups.

Let's look at an example. Animals that eat meat are part of the order Carnivora. Catlike carnivores are put into the family called Felidae, which has two subfamilies. These subfamilies

A house cat has the scientific name *Felis catus*.

CLASSIFYING A HOUSE CAT

Classification	Name	Characteristics	Examples
Domain	Eukarya	Organisms made of cells with one nucleus	Protists, bacteria, fungi, plants, and animals
Kingdom	Animalia	Organisms that move and cannot make their own food	Fish, birds, insects, worms, reptiles, and humans
Phylum	Chordata	Animals that have a backbone	Fish, birds, reptiles, and humans
Class	Mammalia	Animals that breathe air, are warm-blooded, have hair, and feed milk to their young	Lions, horses, whales, dogs, and humans
Order	Carnivora	Animals that eat meat	Lions, whales, and dogs
Family	Felidae	Cat family	Lions, tigers, jaguars, leopards, cougars, cheetahs, and house cats
Genus	*Felis*	Small cats	Sand cats, wildcats, Chinese mountain cats, and house cats
Species	*catus*		House cats

are broken down into smaller groups. Each of these groups is called a **genus**. Under the genus are all the species that fit within it. The genus *Felis* includes the species domestic cat, sand cat, and wildcat.

Sorting the World

Classifying and sorting living things helps us make sense of the world. It is not always simple, and scientists do not always agree on how to group things.

It is simple to classify some living things, such as whether a plant is a rose bush or a pine tree like the ones these kids are carrying. As scientists learn more about other living things, they often have different ideas on how to classify them.

For a long time, scientists grouped living things into just two kingdoms, plants and animals. As the tools for studying living things improved, scientists learned more about living things. This caused them to change their classification system. As scientists make new discoveries about living organisms, they may suggest either changing organisms' classification or changing the classification system.

GLOSSARY

adapt (uh-DAPT) To change to fit new conditions.

class (KLAS) A group of living things with similar traits.

decomposers (dee-kum-POH-zerz) Living things that break down the cells of dead plants and animals into simpler parts.

genus (JEE-nus) The scientific name for a group of living things that are alike.

nucleus (NOO-klee-us) The center inside a cell that holds the cell's makeup and controls how the cell works.

organisms (OR-guh-nih-zumz) Living beings made of dependent parts.

oxygen (OK-sih-jen) A gas that has no color, taste, or odor and is necessary for people and animals to breathe.

parasites (PER-uh-syts) Living things that live in, on, or with other living things.

photosynthesis (foh-toh-SIN-thuh-sus) The way in which green plants make their own food from sunlight, water, and a gas called carbon dioxide.

reproduce (ree-pruh-DOOS) To make more of something or to have babies.

species (SPEE-sheez) A single kind of living thing. All people are one species.

spores (SPORZ) Special cells that can grow into new living things.

vascular (VAS-kyuh-lur) Having a system of tubes that carry liquid.

INDEX

WEB SITES

Due to the changing nature of Internet links, PowerKids Press has developed an online list of Web sites related to the subject of this book. This site is updated regularly. Please use this link to access the list:
www.powerkidslinks.com/lels/class/